CABANATUAN

A PRISONER'S PERSPECTIVE

JOHN F. BATCHELER
SHELLY E. MCCANDLISS

ISBN-13: 978-1724227119
ISBN-10: 1724227114

DEDICATION

For every man and woman who have served for our
freedom. Thank you with all of my heart.

CONTENTS

ACKNOWLEDGMENTS

Thank you, mom, for passing down Grandpa's rich history to us. After all you have been through, you are an incredibly gracious, kind and generous woman.

MY GRANDFATHER

AS I PUT THIS BOOK together, I am overcome with tears and gratitude. I live peacefully and free because of what so many went through for me and for my family.

My Grandpa John was a prisoner of war at Camp No.1, Cabanatuan in the Philippines from 1942 to 1945. There are films and writings depicting the atrocities later challenged as war crimes from that time in the Philippines. I cannot imagine, even with the films' help, what it would have been like to live through what my grandpa and thousands of others did for so long.

My grandfather, John F. Batcheler, was born in Boston, Massachusetts in 1912. He was the first of his family line to be born in the United States. His father was from England and his mother from Scotland. His sisters, Kay and Gladys, were both born in London before they moved, while John was born two years after they came to America.

My grandfather joined the Army Air Corps as a machinist in 1935 when he was 23 years old. He served for 10 years. He knew so little of what those 10 years would hold for him.

Grandpa John married Lucille, my grandmother, in 1939. She was just 18 years old. They met at Moffett Field where John and her father were both stationed. They lived in Menlo Park, California. It was only two years after they married that he would become a prisoner of war.

Technical Sargent John F. Batcheler of 24th Pursuit Group, 21st Pursuit Squadron, would spend three hellish years in the Philippines. His epic started at Clark Field, then Nichols Field, south of Manila on the island of Luzon. It was at Nichols field where he was wounded by shrapnel during an air raid. He became quite ill with Malaria, Dysentery, and hunger over the weeks following. Suffering from his wound and illness, he was brought to Fort Mills Hospital on Corregidor, a tiny island south of the Bataan Peninsula. This island held General MacArthur's Headquarters.

When Corregidor fell on May 6th, 1942, John's time as a prisoner of war began. He was struggling with arthritis, malnutrition and beriberi. He spent about 2 months in the Fort Mills Hospital "Tunnel." John writes in his war statement upon returning home, "Tunnel life as a patient was a nightmare. With no help in view, the island was ordered to surrender, and as prisoners of war nearly the entire garrison was herded into the 'Hole' as we called it, where filth and flies clung to practically every inch of every body, alive or dead. It was a taste of 'life' to come for the next three years." He said the stench of dysentery and gangrene was unbearable.

After two months in the Hole, John and the rest of

the prisoners were transferred by barge to Bilibid Prison south of Manila. They had to walk eight miles from the dock to the prison, stand in the rain for 2 hours, and finally brought into the administrative building to try and sleep. At 4:30 the next morning they were transferred in overstuffed rail cars, with untouchable, hot steel sides, north towards Cabanatuan. They were packed in 100 per boxcar, which were 1/3 the size of our typical boxcar. It was standing room only, so close they couldn't bend their knees. They were forced to go to the bathroom where they were standing. John had passed out twice from nausea and lack of food and water. He said, "The odor of feces was heavy in the air, and we were never more grateful for anything than the opportunity to tumble out of that box and find we really were at Cabanatuan."

From the rail station in the town of Cabanatuan, they were forced to walk nine more miles to Camp 1, though sick and hungry. "The end of the march came at last in a barbed wire enclosure about ¾ of a mile long and five hundred yards wide. It was an old

Philippine Army training camp, half constructed only in the case of many of the buildings. There were already about seven thousand men inside, consisting of prisoners from both Bataan and Corregidor. I saw once more several men from my own squadron for the first time since April and before. This was our home, for almost three years for many of us, and became known as Prison Camp No. 1, Cabanatuan, Philippine Islands."

"We were ordered to line up in rows, our meager possessions on the ground in front of us. The inspection was carried out in the most insulting manner possible. Possession of an article of any value brought the prisoner a few slaps across the face and confiscation of whatever it would be. After the Japanese had enjoyed their game, it was about dark, they left us. We were at last official guests of 'Cabbage Town' as Cabanatuan became known to us."

"At the beginning of prison life in April, May and June of 1942, not a man among us escaped the ravages of malnutrition (represented by scurvy, pellagra, beriberi and many cases of blindness or partial loss of sight), malaria, dysentery, bronchial and chest troubles. Some men, myself included, suffered with all of these ailments at one time. Medicine, except small amounts of Japanese Quinine and a few supplies brought along by our own Medical officers, was refused us. The death rate climbed from twenty-five to thirty a day and up to sometimes as high as forty-five a day. Pleas for more food and a chance to improve our living conditions reached deaf ears. A Japanese regulation prohibited the alteration of buildings or the construction of anything that would result in more personal comfort. Latrines were mere open slits in the ground, breeding flies by the millions. The heavy rains formed one large mud hole of the entire camp area, yet it was months before we were allowed to construct our own drainage system, a series of crisscrossing ditches, to drain off only the surplus water. A tropical rain can be a deluge for days at a time, and under these conditions they purposely designated our 'cemetery' area as the lowest spot possible just outside the camp area. The latter consisted of common burial holes; about twenty feet square and barely deep enough to partially cover many of the bodies, laid in tightly side-by-side like cordwood. I have gone on burial details myself when, in order to reach the day's 'grave,' we had to carry our dead on bamboo mats across and through ankle-deep mud, blood and filth."

"Punishment for infraction of camp rules varied with the whim of the Japanese guards and officers. In the mildest form, it consisted of several slaps across the face, or blows on the shins or across the back with anything at hand, rifle butt, bayonet or a pole. Perhaps the infraction was against a regulation prohibiting the eating of food on the farm, or for not saluting a guard (necessary upon meeting a Japanese guard of any rank), no matter what the crime, the punishment could be serious enough to hospitalize the recipient with broken bones or at best severe cuts and bruises. We were also constantly threatened with cuts in the amount of rations, a punishment which occurred at least an even dozen times during my stay at Cabanatuan. Death was the punishment for approaching the barbed wire closer than three meters, but one American officer was shot from the tower by a guard for working on a small garden he had planted a good ten meters from the fence. The first shot only wounded him, so when he attempted to crawl to safety he was instantly killed by a second shot. He had no warning and was way within his rights, yet Japanese headquarters upheld the guard and the camp as a whole received a cut in rations. Mass punishment was their particular pet method and was usually all out of proportion to the so-called 'injustice' due to the Japanese military. Punishment for escape was death. If one man escaped, the remaining nine of the ten-man 'escape squads' we were always organized under, were shot. Such stories as I have related could fill a book, so I shall dwell upon this no longer."

At Camp Cabanatuan, he and the rest of the prisoners continued to be treated cruelly, as was custom to the Japanese style at that time.

In my grandfather's story you will learn more of what his years at Camp 1 entailed, but you will also learn of another perspective from his time there. This perspective shows us the character of my grandfather and it is a story worth sharing.

I want to say to all of you who have served for our country, I am in awe of what you have done for all of us. I want to represent the American people who have never served, or have not had someone close to them serve in the military for our country. We will never know what you went through. It is hard for us to understand and truly empathize with your incredible experience and sacrifice, what you saw, or what you had to do. I'm so sorry for not knowing how to truly appreciate your gift to us. I'm sorry for not knowing how to talk to you, listen to you, or how to treat you. I'm so sorry for every way that we have misunderstood or mistreated you. Please forgive us.

How do we say thank you enough? On behalf of my family, I want to say thank you for all that you did for the American people. What a sacrificial gift you have given. We are forever grateful to you.

The following is my grandfather's short story, "The Good Samaritan at Cabanatuan." It is a true story from his experience in the prisoner camp at Cabanatuan. It is the part he chose to retell, to relive.

THE GOOD SAMARITAN OF
CABANATUAN

John F. Batcheler

FROG EYES

BEING A PRISONER OF WAR is no life one would voluntarily choose, yet it affords a rare sideline view of war's turbulent backwash. In the shadows of its prison compounds, the true stamp and moral weave of humankind can be vividly revealed in the pathos and drama that play itself out. Sometimes, what you see isn't pretty. Yet here and there you find someone to renew your faith in man's fundamental sense of goodwill. Such a man was Frog Eyes.

The first time I saw him was early in World War II. In that first glimpse he was a mere worm's-eye view of a Japanese guard, wearing thick-lensed glasses and a toothy grin. The view was from the hot, dry dust of a country road in the Philippines, looking straight up. I had fallen there only moments before, utterly spent and racked with fever. Mercifully, the shadow of his round face had intervened to din the incessant rays of the sun. That baleful eye had hovered over Nueva Eoija Province for what seemed like an eternity of hours. How many hours, I did not know. Nor did I care right then. That blessed wetness on my lips was water.

Strangely, I remembered then something I had said back when this was just beginning. Thirst and hunger can play weird tricks on another man's sense of values, and I had unconscionably held mine up to heaven as barter for one cool glass of water. Values can be cheaply traded when they are the last of many, only too recently trodden under foot. Defeat generates a benumbing bitterness, and Corregidor had fallen to the Japanese not three weeks before. The hell of Bataan was a grizzly memory a month old, and it trailed along beside us that day. We were the last bedraggled Americans being herded into camp.

For a day and a half we had traveled the narrow-gauge rails from Manila's Bilibid Prison to Penaranda. Packed one hundred deep in a freight car is not the most luxurious way to move, but in Penaranda that morning rail construction had forced us to take to the road for the last twenty-nine kilometers. Our destination was Camp No. 1, Cabanatuan, and what was to become 'home' for many of the more (or less?) fortunate of us for the next three years.

THE ROAD

AT FIRST THE JOY OF knowing fresh air, free of the stench of human excretions, revived us almost to the point of buoyancy. But few kilometers on foot are needed to make a malaria-infested and undernourished body wilt under such intolerable heat. The volume steadily stretched into a thin, weary stream prodded on by threat and force. Guarding soon became patently unnecessary, for not one had the strength or the will to attempt escape. It was about then that I had prayed to God I might trade my anguished body for the cold, sweet feeling of water in my throat.

There were some that day who didn't make it through to Cabanatuan. But theirs is a harsh and grievous tale, too often told, and this is but the short account of one who gave a little of what was his, that some within his reach might get through. And not only through that day, but through many of those to come, at his own peril. Though he was by man's rules of war an enemy, there is another law that more fittingly embraces him, and I choose to feel that of his race there were many more such as he. For me, and I know not how many others, there was only him. And he left a mark that began that afternoon as I lay in the dust of a Philippine roadside, with not much of life left to cling to.

I remember hearing a quick voice, somewhere in the distance of a fogged mind. Then the shadowy face was gone, and the sun came down again like a hot iron. And with it came fear and confusion; the same kind of chilling fear I had seen in the eyes of others. A sick prisoner is only an unaccommodating trouble, to be gotten rid of, yet why then had there been water?   That   wasn't   part   of   the   ritual.

The road pressed hot against my hands as I made an effort to rise. Half up, a world full of Cogon grass and rice paddies danced wildly before my eyes, and then something firm but oddly gentle pressed my shoulders to the ground. A hand raised my head, and through a mist I saw the face again, closer this time. Something hard forced upon my lips. Moist coolness coursed down my throat. Greedily I seized at its source, but all too suddenly it was gone.

Thinly then in the distance, there was the sound of a voice. It was a man's voice, but it didn't quite belong, I thought. Not all of it; something was wrong. It spoke English.

"No more! Takusan water!" he said brusquely, and through glazed eyes I saw him stand, peering into the distance. In a moment he was bending over me once more, pointing animatedly down the road.

"All gone," he waved, indicating the rest had moved on. And then sharply, "You wait. Very soon, be back."

Hazily I remember him fumbling with his headgear.

Something wet covered my face, shutting him of from sight; and then nothing.

SWEET REST

HOW LONG I REMAINED unconscious I do not know. Slowly my senses returned, and out of somewhere I knew a jarring pressure at my back. Strident, grating sounds across from beneath, at irregular intervals. It was some time before I realized I was lying in the bed of a cart. I stirred cautiously, not knowing what to expect, and discovered from the feel and the sweetish smell that I was laying on a layer of sugar cane. More of it covered my body, except for a damp rag which lay across my face.

Warily I removed the cover from my eyes, and rose to my elbows. I felt stronger, and the sun seemed less intense. The cart, I noticed, was a native carabao wagon, and on the seat sat an elderly Filipino woman. Walking beside the wagon was Frog Eyes, and my movements launched him immediately into agitated motioning.

"Down!" he ordered sharply. "Kuda!" Quickly, I did as he said, but not before noticing that the cover on my face had been the cloth neckpiece from his headgear. I held it in my hand, studying its course, brown weave, and wondered how far he had walked in that sun without its protection. And wondering, too, why he was doing this. It wasn't that kind of a war. Not till now, at least.

Beneath the cane it was almost cold, for the fever had broken during unconsciousness. Soon I sensed darkness coming on, and once there was the woman's voice above me, and an answer from beside the wagon. Other than that there was only the steady creaking of the wheels, and the blurred passage of time. A fitful but grateful sleep finally overtook me.

MY ARRIVAL

THE GOLDEN HUES OF ASIAN twilight were
filling the horizon when Frog Eyes brought the
wagon to a stop. Wordlessly he pulled aside the cane,
and excitedly motioned me to hurriedly get down. He
waved the woman on, still without words, and
indicated to me with a commanding gesture a point
some five hundred yards down the road. It was a
sprawling group of Nipa Grass shacks, and only then
did I realize the extent to which he had gone to give
me succor, and the reason for his nervous silence.
This was Cabanatuan, and were his superiors to learn
of his actions on my behalf his fate would be quick, if

not merciful.

I turned for a moment and looked at him, standing there inscrutably before me, a new and almost menacing look in his eyes. Outwardly at least, he was once more the Japanese guard. But I knew, as he did, that the threatening gestures with his rifle were only a protective cover against discovery. I placed his neckpiece in his hand, still wet from his own canteen, and quickly started up the road as he had ordered, a renewed strength in my walk.

We turned in where a narrow lane divided the cap in two. A gate centered on the prison compound, and it was towards this that I was unceremoniously prodded. Altogether it was an admirable performance on the part of my escort, to the delight of his buddies in the guard quarters across from the American side of camp. But, except perhaps for a little apprehension within him and a measure of weariness on my own part, no one enjoyed that moment more than Frog Eyes and me.

A final and almost lovable foot on my posterior sent

me 'reeling' through the gate. I turned on one knee and glanced through the barbed wire, hoping by some small sign to show the gratitude I felt. But he was already striding away, his short, stocky body growing dim in the gathering dusk. It was as if he were saying he didn't need my thanks; he had done what he had wanted to do, at no man's command.

This ended my first encounter with Frog Eyes. How and where he first came by the name, no one ever knew, and it was a name I was not to know him by for some time to come. He and his stubby spectacles faded into the dreary limbo of prison routine, and it was many months before I saw him again.

CABANATUAN

LIFE AT CABANATUAN BECAME a desolate procession of days, with hunger and disease our constant companions. For some time the death rate hovered between thirty and forty a day, chopping steadily away at the original ten thousand Americans housed in the compound. It continued so on into August of 1942, when the turn of fate swung somewhat the other way. Then came the rains.

As the first Christmas drew near there seemed little to be thankful for. Hammering winds and rain swept clean some of the signs of filth and desolation, but minds and bodies were becoming stupefyingly reconciled to constant suffering. With ominous portent there came a dangerous spreading of the most deadly disease of all, the will to die. What few men there were from my own outfit, the 21st Pursuit Squadron, frequently gathered in failing efforts to maintain our own flagging spirits. Most poignant of all was the hope medicine would find its way in, to stave off the inroads of beriberi and dysentery.

The days moved on into December, and more and more there was the furtive mention of someone by the name of Frog Eyes. Sometimes, but not always, death was forestalled by the mysterious appearance of a small handful of medicine. Whispered warnings against any acknowledgement of it always accompanied its delivery, and it always came at night. Few enough benefited from the mystic underground, but the sparks of hope it created left upon those few an indelible mark.

It was during the tail end of a particularly heavy storm that I was assigned to the nightly guard shift at my barracks. The howling winds slanting rain were gradually dying out, and I was huddled just inside the barracks' entrance (there were no doors) waiting to see whether the Japanese Officer of the Day would make the rounds. It hardly seemed likely that he would, for the camp was a quagmire, the darkness almost solid.

The ship's bell near the center of camp had just struck eight bells, and I had about decided to crawl under my soggy blanket and try to sleep when I heard the sound of splashing footsteps picking their way along the camps central pathway, and then I lost them in the tearing wind.

Low voices came to ma during a lull in the storm, from the front of adjacent barracks. One a Japanese voice. A startlingly familiar sound. I'd heard it speak only a half a dozen words, only once before, but it was enough.

A light blinked once, glistening against the slanting rain, and then I was sure. Those thick lensed glasses were a tell tale sign. Without thinking, I stepped into the blackness of the pathway, heading cautiously across the intervening space. Somewhere part way there was a blurred figure, and a hand touched my arm. Something was forced into my grasp, and I recognized the voice of an American.

"For Whitey. You know what to do." Then he was gone. Inside, Whitey was on the verge of death, and I knew what it was I held in my hand. And I knew, too, who Frog Eyes really was.

THE LAST 500

THE NEXT MORNING BROKE clear and warm. Those of us able enough gathered near the gate for daily work details. Before leaving, I searched for the American who had spoken to me the night before and took him aside.

"He shouldn't have come himself last night," I said, having heard that he never did so. "It's dangerous."

"It was necessary," was the answering shrug. "How's Whitey?"

"He's dead," I answered. "There'll be someone else who can use it," he said bitterly, as he turned and walked away.

The months drew into years. Many of the physically able were shipped to Japan and Manchuria. I saw Frog Eyes only once after that, and for some time I knew that he had been transferred from the guard detail. He came back in December of 1944, and it was then that I saw him on the prison farm. There was a limp to his walk then, and American guns could be heard blasting their way down from Linguyan Gulf. Only the least fit could be spared from the Japanese lines to guard the five hundred remaining in the camp.

At seven o'clock on the night of January 30, 1945, the quiet of the camp was ruptured by a hail of gunfire. Sixth Army rangers and Filipino guerillas closed in from two sides. Tanks and bazookas made a holocaust of the Japanese area. We were herded through a cut in the barbed wire. As I walked outside that fence for the last time, I couldn't resist looking back over my shoulder at the inferno on the hillside. Somewhere in that flaming rain was Frog Eyes. Unless God willed it, otherwise his own life was right

Enemy though he was, a quiet prayer formed on my lips in his behalf, as I stepped across the road to freedom. It was the very same road up which he had dutifully marched me three years before.

The End.

SURVIVED

ONLY ABOUT 500 MEN MADE it through the tragic three years at Cabanatuan. At its peak, the camp held about 10,000 Americans. Some were shipped out on hell ships to Japan. Most of those soldiers did not survive their time on the ships because of terrible holding conditions with a lack of oxygen and sanitation, overwhelming heat, lack of food and water, and multiple illnesses. Some of the ships were even sunk by allied torpedoes not knowing the POW's were on board. Thousands at the camp died of malnutrition and illnesses the Japanese guards could have tended to. At one point fellow prisoners were burying 45-50 soldiers a day. Death was relentless.

On January 30, 1945, The Great Raid took place. Redemption so swift, it is a story to hear over and over again. It was the single most successful raid in US history. My grandfather wrote, "Five hundred and eleven of us were liberated from Camp No.1, Cabanatuan, on the night of January 30, 1945, by the Sixth Army Rangers. At approximately seven o'clock on the evening of that day, the firing of machine guns and bazookas seemingly on all sides of the camp, made us 'hit the ground'. The front lines of the American advance into Luzon was only twenty-five miles away, and we had had a feeling for two or three weeks that we would either be massacred or killed on masse for 'attempting to escape'. We figured the firing was for that purpose until after about five minutes we were told by a voice in the dark to 'head for the gate'. We did so without further hesitation, except those of us bedridden. They were carried out and placed in Caribou wagons. The camp was cleared in twenty-five minutes, after a perfectly timed break by the Rangers and Philippine Guerrilla. Two Rangers were killed and one wounded, but no casualties occurred among the prisoners. We marched approximately twenty-five miles that night, most of us shoeless, arriving at the American lines, passing through the Japanese' at dawn."

You can watch the rescue mission on film (The Great Raid, 2005), or read of many accounts and memorials. Thank you, Heroes, for rescuing those 500.

My grandpa was one of the few that survived. I wouldn't be here had he not made it out. We have two boys, Brennan and Caleb, whom we adopted at birth. I was sharing this with Brennan (14 years old), "Bud, if Grandpa John had not made it out, you boys would still be here but you wouldn't be our sons. I wouldn't be here." And he said, "Caleb wouldn't be my brother. I wouldn't even know him." We just stared at each other. The thought was sobering. We are so grateful for Grandpa John making it through such a terrible time. I am so thankful to the man, "Frog Eyes", for helping my grandfather.

I wish I could have known my grandfather as an adult but he passed away when I was just a child. I had no idea what he had gone through. I would have loved to talk with him, listen to him, and thank him. He had been through so much and had so many injustices done to him. I find it amazing the part of the story he wanted to share was some of the good of his enemy. And he chose to believe it wasn't just Frog Eyes who had a heart to help.

As I did hours and hours of research on the history of this portion of the war, it began to weigh heavy on my heart how one race could treat another race so cruelly. The stories of how the Japanese must have viewed the soldiers to be able to behead some and parade the decapitation around like a victory march, to beat the men while they are down on the ground, to burry men alive, or withhold food, water, or medicine to the sick and dying is barbaric. It is hard for me to comprehend.

HOW DO WE HEAL?

I PERSONALLY HAVE HAD SOME difficult injustices in my life. I was sexually abused as a child, my parents were divorced when I was young, my mother married three more times after that, moving us over 20 times throughout my childhood. I do not know what you have gone through, so I offer the following humbly. It has helped me gain peace and freedom from the past so I am able to be more fully alive in the present.

When injustices happen, each of us reacts differently. Regardless to the style of response, these injustices affect us negatively, continually, until we take care of their roots. The anger we might struggle with, the unshakable depression, are examples of how injustices continue to plague us. We don't have to live with those strongholds, no matter how terrible our past is.

The most powerful tool against injustices is forgiveness. You don't have to feel like it, just want it. You don't have to include the other person in the forgiveness process, and most importantly, it does not excuse what they did to you. Forgiveness is for your heart and your health, not for them. There are multiple studies on how sick people get well after forgiving someone. It has also been the tool that has brought me the most freedom in my life. I am a whole and healthy person because of the work of forgiveness I have had the opportunity to do.

The reason we are able to forgive is because God forgave us. He made a beautiful world that we have wrecked in so many ways. Then He sent the plan to redeem us, Jesus. Jesus died for us so we don't have to. We can have life with Him that is powerful because He rose from the dead, conquering the enemy. Now we too can have that power against the enemy's plans to drag us down because of injustices. Jesus is the reason we can forgive anyone at all. He is the Way because He's the one that made everything. If you designed the board game Monopoly, you get to say how to win the game. The creator of the game isn't egocentric, biased, or closed-minded because he made one way to win, he just made it that way. God created all that is good. He provided the way to the finish line, Jesus Christ. . If you do not know Him as your Savior and would like to, I can lead you in that now.

Dear Jesus, I am sorry for living my life without you. I'm sorry for my bad choices. Thank you so much for forgiving me, for dying on the cross to rescue me. I let all of that go and I choose now for you to be Lord of my life. I want to follow you and be close to you. Thank you Jesus. Amen.

If you just prayed that prayer, asking Him to be God in your life, please find someone to tell who will encourage you and walk with you on your new journey. I have another book that can help you in this new life, The Brady Letters. It is an interactive journal to help activate you towards more freedom, hearing God's voice, and closeness with Him.

Now you have the authority to break any bad patterns of attitude or decisions that are affecting you. When you forgive, you get the power back to be in charge of your own emotions and choices. For instance, if I did not forgive the Japanese people of the past, I would start a dark system in my mind, and in my heart, that would only grow. As it grows, that system would take away more of my power to make good decisions or be a healthy human being, until I eventually choose to forgive them.

Now I want to give you the opportunity to walk through forgiving those who have wronged you and caused injustices in your life. I'm going to use some examples of injustices of war as the focus, but in the blanks you fill in anyone that hurt you or anything else that happened to you. Remember, you don't have to feel like it; you just have to decide you want freedom from the effects of the injustice and go for it. The perpetrator doesn't have any part of this. It does not excuse what they did to you; it is simply freedom for you.

Lord, I forgive ________________________________
(The Race you had to fight that hurt you and those you knew, the Americans who did not understand, yourself, fellow soldiers or authorities, your spouse, etc.) for ________________________________
(list everything they did to hurt you).

Lord, I release these people from owing me anything and I bless them with a rich life, salvation, joy, health, and love.

Father, I repent for ________________________________
(this is where you repent for all ways you've been affected by the injustices, reacting negatively; anger, bitterness, unforgiveness, alienating yourself, closing down, depression, oppression, apathy, etc.)

Thank you, Jesus, for forgiving me. I am free from this sin because of your acceptance and gift of grace to me. Thank you Lord.

By the power of the Blood of Jesus, I rebuke those negative behaviors from being strongholds in my life. I say with full authority, "No More, In Jesus' Name!", and I break off all trauma from my past now! I cut the tether and let it loose. Trauma can have no more affect on me. I disagree with it now, in Jesus' powerful name.

I am a free person now; free to love and be loved, free to be whole and a gift to those around me. I am courageous, patient, loving, generous, strong, brave, significant, joyful, trusting, and healthy. Amen.

This prayer can be done using different situations as you remember them, as often as you need to. We have been through a lot in our lives. We might not remember it all at once but as things come up, and as new injustices come to our lives, this tool will be continually useful.

I am going to give an example from my own life and walk through the prayer for myself regarding the captors that held my grandfather.

Lord, I forgive the Japanese guards in the Philippines. I forgive them for treating my grandfather, and thousands of others as trash and not as human beings. I forgive them for their lack of honor, for withholding medicine and food, for beating them and being consistently irrational. I release them from owing me, or my grandfather, anything and I bless them and their children with wholeness, salvation, love, and joy in their lives. I am so sorry for my anger towards them, for thinking so little of them for what they did. Thank you for forgiving me for my anger and judgment. I rebuke anger and judgment now, in Jesus' name. It is no longer mine. I am a loving child of God who sees others through the eyes of her Father. Thank you Lord. Amen.

That's it. It doesn't have to be long and drawn out. Jesus died on the cross so we could have the authority to access freedom for our lives. It's more about Him than us. Another helpful tip, one that will help you hold onto the forgiveness you gave, is to train yourself to no longer talk badly about those you have forgiven. The Lord has them and will deal with the injustices far better than we ever could. Romans 12:19 says, "Do not take revenge, my dear friends, but leave room for God's wrath, for it is written: 'It is mine to avenge; I will repay,' says the Lord."

I bless your journey to be rich with Him. You are valuable, a priceless treasure to Him. He loves you more than you will ever be able to comprehend.

In Jeremiah 31:3, God says, "I have loved you with an everlasting love; I have drawn you with unfailing kindness."

The only other positive thing I read in all of my research besides my grandfather's story, had to do with the sunsets at Camp 1, Cabanatuan. Some of the prisoners described the sunsets as something pretty incredible. One man shared, "The Sunsets are magnificent. I doubt if they can be duplicated anywhere." They said that men used to pause at that time of the evening to watch them.

The sun kept rising and setting for all of us.

But it was more beautiful for them.

A NOTE FOUND

AS MY MOTHER SEARCHED through boxes to find information and memories of my grandfather, she came across a note he wrote me when I was born.

October 21, 1972

My Dear Rachelle,

Today has a very special meaning. One month ago you were born, to fill the hearts of your Mom and Dad with pride and to bless the lives of all of us with your presence.

Too often we take for granted the wondrous

gift of life. And so in the years to come, when you read this, may you know that you have helped us all to see its true meaning a little clearer by coming to us – a perfect little baby girl, where such a short time ago you were just a hoped-for dream. Thus this small gift of love and affection to say thank you.

May you know the blessing of a full life, rich with the greatest treasure of all – sharing; the giving and receiving of ourselves in the warm-hearted togetherness of sincere laughter and love, in an atmosphere of trust and faith. There is no purer joy. May your heart sing with it. Always.

Your loving grandfather,

John Batcheler